Yes I'd Love to Dance

Maggie O'Dwyer

Templar Poetry

First Published 2008 by Templar Poetry
Templar Poetry is an imprint of Delamide & Bell

Fenelon House,
Kingsbridge Terrace
58 Dale Road, Matlock, Derbyshire
DE4 3NB

www.templarpoetry.co.uk

ISBN 978-1-906285-22-7

Copyright © Maggie O'Dwyer 2008

Maggie O'Dwyer has asserted her right to be identified
as the author of this work in accordance
with the Copyright, Designs and Patents Act 1988.

All rights reserved. This book is sold subject to the condition
that it shall not, by way of trade or otherwise, be lent, resold, hired out
or otherwise circulated without the publisher's prior consent, in any form
of binding or cover other than that in which it is published and without
a similar condition including this condition being imposed on
the subsequent purchaser.

For permission to reprint or broadcast these poems write to
Templar Poetry

A CIP catalogue record for this book is available from the British Library

Typeset by Pliny
Graphics by Paloma Violet
Printed and bound in Turkey

For Gerry

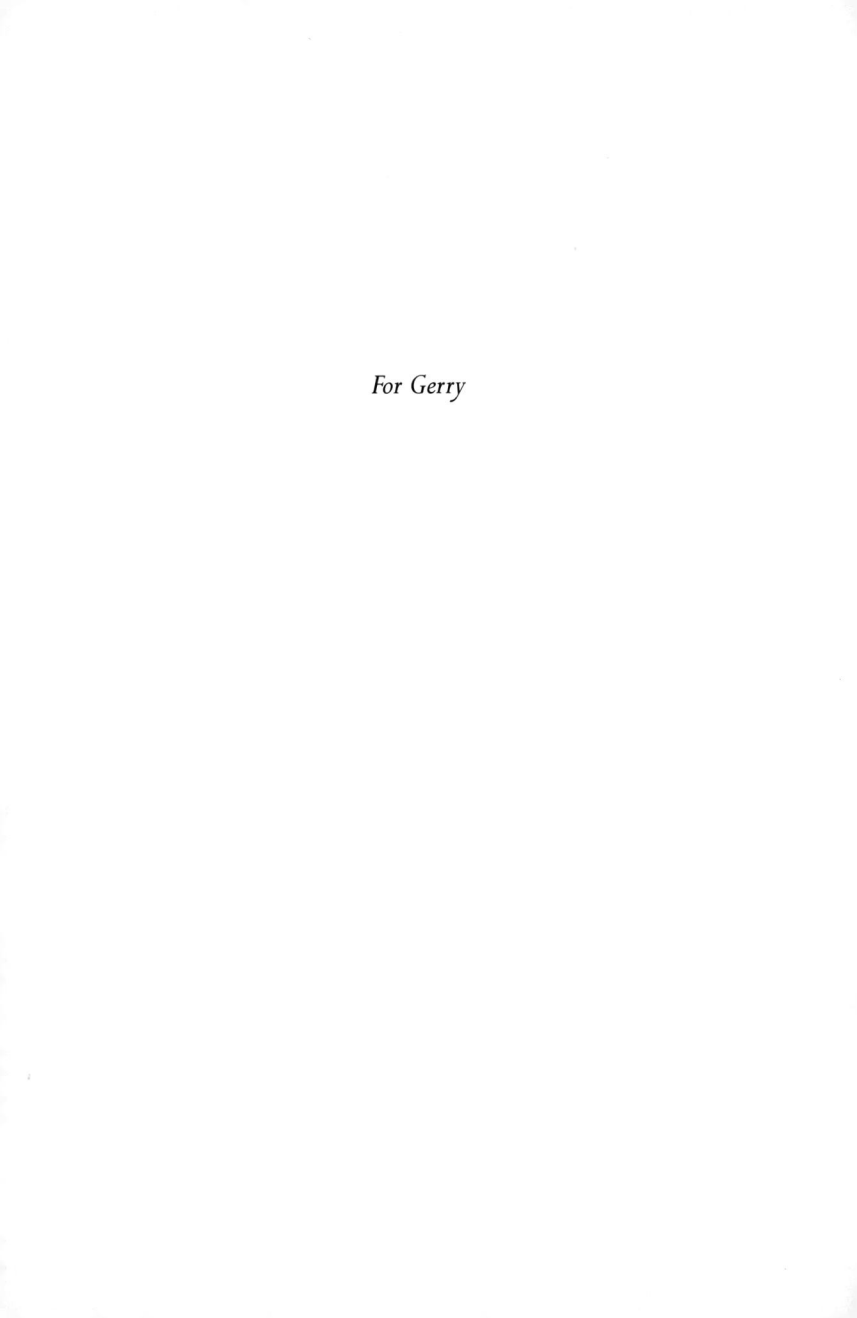

Acknowledgements

Thanks are due to the editors of the following, in which some of these poems have appeared: *The Shop, Piqué (Templar Poetry), Thornfield - Poems by the Thornfield Poets, (Salmon Poetry).*

Special thanks to the late Dorothy Molloy, the members of Thornfield Poets. Particular thanks to Ivy Bannister, Celia de Fréine and Louise C. Callaghan, my family and friends, James J. McAuley for his workshops, Isobel McMahon, Alex McMillen for his constant encouragement, and very special thanks to Gerry.

Contents

Once upon a time	1
The Pictures	2
Pamplona	4
Cadence	6
Missing	7
The Poet of Baghdad	8
Blood	10
Imprint	11
The Last Time	12
For Tipperary Maggie from Timbuktu Ted	13
Yo creo en la libertad / *I believe in freedom*	14
I won't let go even though	15
Wallflowers	16
All Dressed Up	18
The Handkerchief Tree	19
She Is Water	20
Blocked Gutters	22
Not Falling This Time	23
Body	26
Take The Sedative	28
Yes, I'd love to dance	30
I Ching	32
I Do	33

Once upon a time

Nights you're away, the amaryllis opens
like an underskirt of silk, ruffled red.
Time hangs on its petals,
the grass prepares itself for frost.
I stay up way past my bedtime, to out wake
my cluttered dreams, blow out the smoke
from another cigarette.
On the TV, a man tells his story of love
and on another channel, a woman tells hers.
It begins…

The Pictures

It begins with a mood
snow perhaps or mist
something dreamy.
The colour is faded
has the sound
of a cello, or voices
keening.
It depends of course
on where it happens
west would be blue,
east yellow.
There's slow motion,
a young man falls in blue,
a woman sinks to her knees
in yellow.

Afterwards they fall
inside you
like smooth cold milk,
you can't separate
the colour from the sound.
It seems right and wrong
this feeling, so unfair
yet so fucking beautiful.

Outside it's raining
all that grey and blue.
He puts his arm around you,
you lift your face.
He's a private man
but he kisses you in the street,
because he knows you like it
and you need it.

Pamplona

For Siobhan

There's a storm tonight Maria,
first a shiver of grasses, a hiding
of small birds, then clouds
purple with thunder, folding
the light from wheat fields.

You tie up your hair, the strings
of your apron and serve:
anchovies floating in olive oil,
shot glasses of yogurt
and beetroot.

Your Mama lies in a battered
blue car with a stranger, watches
behind him the fig leaves darken
to sage. The bull skids on a corner,
bashes his hind on a wall.

You hear the scrape of his hooves,
the roar of the crowd, as you serve
chocolate soufflé that opens
and spreads onto the white plate
like warm mud.

Someone has taken your face
Maria and closed it, but a thin
line of love escapes and falls
on your cheek, like a dark
wisp of kisses.

Cadence

My mouth is full of music
and voices that live inside me
like ghosts. They plead in Arabic,
lay out their graves in sand.
A choir of women shake
the blossoms from a pear tree
and in harmony my mother
waves goodbye, my father
sits beside me on that long drive
through the mountains.

All I can do is open my mouth,
all I can hope for is that you hear me
and that somehow I can give you
the sound of a mist and forgiveness
found in a line of trees at twilight.

Missing

He did not know when he left me here
that I would claim it, that my hands
would be a bed for spotted irises,
my feet shift to the sway of bog cotton,
my body tremble under the quiet fall
of a fox's paws.

That I would feel rain, drop by drop.

He did not know that I would be
yellow flagged and wet mossed,
that I would see hawthorn settle
like snow in a distant field, elderflower
spread out, white as bone china.

He did not know that even here
I can smell the scent of your lilies
and that your searching heart
comforts me like a curling fog,
that lifts to a spring morning
and Ligeti's notes, caught
in the throat of a skylark's song.

The Poet of Baghdad

Soon it will be dark, the blue plastic string
of the washing line will disappear, the smooth
stone sky. The spaces in between will merge,
the last pear, the flip of a yellow leaf.
I smoke a cigarette, listen to the room

settle into dusk, the hiss of the gas fire.
Is it luck or karma I ask myself,
that gives me the time to watch the evening
curl in on itself, like a black cat?
I could be somewhere else. I could be you.

I don't know how you do it, or how you wear
that ridiculous hat that looks like a shower cap.
How can you stand the heat and all that chatter
in your theatre about the World Cup.
I can see it you know, the way her dress

is blossoming into red, the footprints of blood
on the floor. I can hear the men cry -
They make us feel like women -
and the women scream - *Bring him back.*
Meanwhile, the rivers are bloated

and the breeze is a siren, and I don't know
how you can bear it. How can you bear it?
You say, "scalpel" and when you cut you say,

"Opal, morning, water stirred
by the wing of an azure bird."

Blood

He will not leave his mammy
and she will not leave her daddy
for his mammy and her daddy
don't get on. Her daddy says
she'd be better off with a blanket
and his mammy says
he'd never get fed. Only glances
then, long as shadows.

They die, of course, his mammy
and her daddy and now
he won't leave his house
and she won't leave hers.
The grass grows long between them
and from his house and hers
every evening they watch
the light leak out of the sky.

Imprint

In between the recipes
for eggless, milkless cake
and green gooseberry jam,
I follow the slant of your hand
that wrote "sucks" and "cows,"
"heifers sold" and "profits made"
then "clear" written across the page
in strong upright strokes.
On the torn newspaper recipe
for *strawberries in a Pressure Cooker,*
I see the red imprint of your lips
across the fold.

The Last Time

I always mean to say goodbye,
I always want to, but sometimes
I'm late, or I just can't make it.
Then I'm left with the time before,
yesterday, the last time
and I may not have behaved
all that well, that last time.

I may have kissed the air
around you, allowed my mind
to wander back to myself.
I may even have been bored,
slipped out for a cup of tea,
wondered, if you could possibly
ruin my holiday plans.

I always meant to say I love you,
I always wanted to,
but we weren't brought up that way.
Tell me, are you still wearing
that coat?
I keep seeing you, everywhere.

For Tipperary Maggie from Timbuktu Ted

I have a small room,
a white wash-hand basin,
a Van Gogh chair
and on sunny days
a rectangle of yellow
on my bed.
I have the sound of rain,
pigeons, church bells
and from the horizontal
a film of moods, with
or without clouds.

I have an album full
of photographs of women
snapped in the light
of Sacre Coeur or shaded
in the Jardin des Plantes.
I like to bring them
up to my room, lie beside
them on my narrow bed.
I only kiss the ones
who want to be kissed,
tell stories to the ones
who want to forget.

Yo creo en la libertad / *I believe in freedom*

I've left the clothes in the washing machine,
I haven't hoovered the stairs, e-mailed,
entered a competition or sent out a poem
and the last one I wrote doesn't belong to me any more.
I'm on the road where the fields are seen and hidden
and the light is flat and pale as the flowers of elderberry
and I don't know why, but in between the soar
of *Andrés Jiménez's* voice and the sun trying so hard
to get out, I see myself lean towards you,
I hear someone say, "Hold on, hold on."
I put my lips to your ear, to a place I never kissed
and whisper, "It's okay to go if you want to."

I won't let go even though

I am tired of smoking, the constant
lift to my lips of rolled paper,
smoke held in my mouth and blown out
like a long sigh. I smoke, I long,
I long for a smoke.
Meanwhile, the dark window is a mirror
I see myself in, and you framed on the fridge
smiling at me in your apron
of merry-go-rounds.

In the night mirror I stab out my cigarette
in a small iron ashtray shaped like a heart.
I write away my ghosts, I do what I am told
whisper your name, seal it in an envelope.
I sit and watch as the edge of absence
seeps through the paper and with my finger
I tear across the fold.

Wallflowers

I was happy there
sex-less in paradise
until he came
with his tongue sharp
as a flick knife
and an apple, rosy-red.
"Taste it ," he said.
Oh, I knew
what he was after,
so I gave it to yer man
instead.
He thought he had me then
but I wouldn't budge.
"Right," he said
slithering off.
"Right yourself," I said
"and good riddance."
I could hear him
all through the night
muttering in the grass.
"I am king.
I am water.
I am fire.
I am falling skin"

I nodded off,
next thing I know
I'm outside the gate
lured by the scent
of wallflowers.
Cunning bastard.

All Dressed Up

Minnie Mouse stands in her plastic pink dress, a gold crown between her large black ears, an ice cream in her white gloved hand. She stands with her back to the window on a wooden table between stones. She's been in the same place for months. A cello gathers winter, a finger presses the same soft note on a piano, a violin pulls the first bluebell spears of spring. Minnie looks inward at reflected patterns, stares at the empty gilded frame of a mirror, an Easter egg box full of kisses and letters, where your ink-drawn monkeys leap from page to page. They say, "Paris is a spent peanut shell without you." Minnie Mouse has missed the only fall of snow, the sliver of each new moon, the naked sky, and if I don't turn her around, she'll miss a thousand clouds, when the pear tree bursts into blossom.

The Handkerchief Tree

Father David said, it looks like
fluttering doves, some say a ghost,
and others, most beautiful in twilight.

I say it looks like her letter, torn
and scattered, fallen bracts of light
outside your door.

She Is Water

I knew when I saw her kneel
in front of your painting
in the middle of the New Year's
party with all those bodies
around her, drinking and shouting,
the small room full of the smell
of Guinness, that I had lost.

She was so mysterious and still
and she had this way with colour
and a way of signing off
with a thousand kisses.
She crept into me,
before I even knew she was there.

I found myself drinking Bancha tea,
slicing my carrots diagonally,
eating brown rice with chopsticks.
I stopped eating tomatoes,
started tying up my hair
with ribbons of magenta.

I learnt about Metal, Fire, Wood,
Earth and Water; and you and I,
we were Metal and Wood.
"Not good," she said, "Not good."

It was only later I wanted to tear
off her hyacinth dress
choke the soft voice that said,
"Friendship is better than love."

Blocked Gutters

for Brad Mehldau, jazz pianist

Brad, the light is fading,
the window was half-open
and now it's closed.
There's a dark sky out there
full with its burden of rain,
even the fox has left
its favourite scrap of sunlight.
I've washed the kitchen floor
and tried not to smoke a cigarette.
We're all half-mad here Brad,
waiting for summer.

And then I play you, up loud.
I watch the rain fall
and nothing seems to matter
now, not even summer.
You're just like the window-cleaner,
Brad, clearing out my gutters.
Up on his ladder with a bucket
of water, he shouts down,
"Listen, can you hear that?"
I put my ear to the drain pipe
and Brad, I can hear it.

Not Falling This Time

Brad, did you ever get my poem?
It's been two years and no word.
The summer came that year, late
and hot, cotton blue skies for days
on end. The whole country went mad,
buying pink loungers, Bar-B-Que sets,
lights to hang on their washing lines.
Next door ate out a lot and by nine
the whole estate was roasting.
I couldn't stick it, couldn't sleep at night.

I wanted to be somewhere else,
on the boreen that led down
to the sea, in the house set back
from the road and that fiery line
of montbretia. I wanted to be asleep
in the room where the lilt of a stream
was a cool pillow or above in the village
where I could stand in the shop that sold
beach balls, wafers and copybooks,
hold that smell of plastic, cream and paper.
And the fox, I wanted the fox,
he was the start of it.

Broke my heart he did, lying around
in every scrap of sunshine he could find
and the colour of him
warm as conkers in the spring grass.
I couldn't keep my eyes off him.
I watched him through the wet spring
with the pear tree in blossom
like an electric light in the dark
thundery room, and the cubs, oh God,
the cubs capering in and out,
getting closer and closer to the house.
I fed them, sure what did I know.

"Ah nothing you can do love, they all
get it you know, pass it on to one another,
it's nature, nasty though", he said, "in the end."
Fuck nature I thought, sorry - but I did.
"Mind you," he said, "they don't seem to get
it on the north side."
In the end I couldn't bear it,
went out the front instead,
sat on the steps, the summer came,
some say it was glorious.
Next summer was a wash out.
Slept well.

"Hey, look, is that a fox I see out there
or a big marmalade cat?"
I'm not looking.
"Ah come on, look, it is a fox."
I look beyond the buds on the pear tree
to a warm colour and the turn of a head.

I heard you were here last year,
but I didn't go to see you.
Sure we've both moved on, haven't we?
I still listen to you though, in the same room
on dark wet days.

Body

Sometimes I hate this house.
I want to sell it, walk right out
into something different.
I'm tired of the magnolia
walls and the way it smells
of smoke.
It wakes me up at night
to listen to all its dreams.
I can't make head nor tail
of them. It's like clingfilm
this house and I never know
when it's going to be hot
or cold.

I've tried everything:
burning sage in its corners,
offerings of salt and water.
I'm a fool to think anyone
would want to buy it.
It's a succubus. I'd get out
if I were you, but you love it
and that amazes me.
When I neglect it you say,
"An artist's time is never wasted."

When I smarten it up,
scrub the bathroom sink,
squeaky clean.
You say, "God isn't it lovely,
it's like a hotel."

Take The Sedative

I have the aconite under my tongue,
the arsenic and rescue remedy
in my bag, I'm lying on my side
with a rubber guard in my mouth.
Piece of cake, I think.
"Four minutes," he says. "Deep breath
going down… now."
When I felt it I knew
I should have taken the sedative,
the trolley, the bed, the cup of tea,
the slice of white toast, the pat
of butter and jam.

I'm still not the better of it,
when I see you downstairs in the cafeteria,
eating a sandwich.
"Jesus, that was quick," you say.
"Can you give me a lift back to work?"

That night you hand me a CD of music
you've compiled for me, songs to cheer me up.
Somewhere over the rainbow
and *The big rock candy mountain,* where
there are cigarette trees and lemonade springs,

and all the dogs have rubber teeth.
On the disc you've drawn a scope.
At the top you've written, "let's see"
and at the bottom, "Wow, it's lovely down here."

Yes, I'd love to dance

I wouldn't wear that coat
if I were you, it's grey
and - God Almighty - feel
the weight. I'd wear white
like the tulips at the end
of the garden, niveous
in the dark, or cerulean
like that tree we see
on our way to work,
the one that makes my heart
stop for a second, twice a day
for a whole month. It looks
like a ball gown made with
icing sugar.

Tomorrow morning I'll bring
a ladder, lean it against the tree,
climb up,
push through its vaulted underskirt
of dark yew-green leaves
right up to my waist
and sit there for hours.
I am not in front of a Range Rover
and behind a Subaru,

there are no election posters.
I am at a ball, the air is full
of jasmine and the tinkled sound
of pink champagne and -
I don't believe it - is that you
I see gliding or floating
towards me in that white shirt
I ironed last week?

I Ching

In this quiet flat, against the pale wall
a plastic clotheshorse stands,
white, with one sock
the colour of crushed mulberries.

On the marble mantlepiece white lilies
in a glass vase, a self-portrait of a man
finely drawn in black ink.

He wears a check dressing gown and slippers,
has two mouths, five protrusions from his head,
a tail, a small potted aloe vera plant at his feet,
three chinese coins in the palm of his hand.

Underneath you have written,
"Le cadeau."

I Do

For Carol and Arthur

I will hold up the sky for you,
give you a bolt of crimson silk,
the scent of cinnamon and thyme
on my fingers, the sound of my
laughter, bright as hay in a field.

I will give you the pale bowed
heads of hellebores, the last
niveous light of winter
and shadows quiet as the leaves
of a pear tree in summer,

and oh my love, when the night
is dark, and the world is lonely,
I will give you my hand on your head,
the moon in a bone china cup,
the unfinished map of myself.